MOVIE FAVORITES

Solos and Band Arrangements
Correlated with Essential Elements Band Method

Arranged by
MICHAEL SWEENEY

Welcome to Essential Elements Movie Favorites! There are two versions of each selection in this versatile book. The SOLO version appears on the left-hand page of your book. The FULL BAND arrangement appears on the right-hand page. Optional accompaniment recordings are available separately in CD or cassette format. Use these recordings when playing solos for friends and family.

ISBN 978-0-7935-5966-4

HAL•LEONARD®
CORPORATION
7777 W. BLUEMOUND RD. P.O. BOX 13819 MILWAUKEE, WI 53213

From The Universal Motion Picture JURASSIC PARK

Theme From "JURASSIC PARK"

KEYBOARD PERCUSSION
Solo

Composed by JOHN WILLIAMS
Arranged by MICHAEL SWEENEY

MCA music publishing

From The Universal Motion Picture JURASSIC PARK

Theme From "JURASSIC PARK"

KEYBOARD PERCUSSION
Band Arrangement

Composed by JOHN WILLIAMS
Arranged by MICHAEL SWEENEY

 **MCA** music publishing

00860022

From CHARIOTS OF FIRE

CHARIOTS OF FIRE

KEYBOARD PERCUSSION
Solo

Music by VANGELIS
Arranged by MICHAEL SWEENEY

00860022

CHARIOTS OF FIRE

KEYBOARD PERCUSSION
Band Arrangement

Music by VANGELIS
Arranged by MICHAEL SWEENEY

00860022

From THE MAN FROM SNOWY RIVER

THE MAN FROM SNOWY RIVER
(Main Title Theme)

KEYBOARD PERCUSSION
Solo

By BRUCE ROWLAND
Arranged by MICHAEL SWEENEY

From **THE MAN FROM SNOWY RIVER**

THE MAN FROM SNOWY RIVER
(Main Title Theme)

KEYBOARD PERCUSSION
Band Arrangement

By **BRUCE ROWLAND**
Arranged by **MICHAEL SWEENEY**

From The Paramount Motion Picture FORREST GUMP

FORREST GUMP - MAIN TITLE
(Feather Theme)

KEYBOARD PERCUSSION
Solo

Music by ALAN SILVESTRI
Arranged by MICHAEL SWEENEY

00860022

From The Paramount Motion Picture FORREST GUMP

FORREST GUMP - MAIN TITLE
(Feather Theme)

KEYBOARD PERCUSSION
Band Arrangement

Music by ALAN SILVESTRI
Arranged by MICHAEL SWEENEY

00860022

From AN AMERICAN TAIL
Somewhere Out There

**Words and Music by JAMES HORNER,
BARRY MANN and CYNTHIA WEIL**
Arranged by MICHAEL SWEENEY

KEYBOARD PERCUSSION
Solo

MCA music publishing

SOMEWHERE OUT THERE

**Words and Music by JAMES HORNER,
BARRY MANN and CYNTHIA WEIL**

Arranged by MICHAEL SWEENEY

KEYBOARD PERCUSSION
Band Arrangement

From DANCES WITH WOLVES

THE JOHN DUNBAR THEME

KEYBOARD PERCUSSION
Solo

By JOHN BARRY
Arranged by MICHAEL SWEENEY

THE JOHN DUNBAR THEME

KEYBOARD PERCUSSION
Band Arrangement

By JOHN BARRY
Arranged by MICHAEL SWEENEY

From The Paramount Motion Picture RAIDERS OF THE LOST ARK

RAIDERS MARCH

KEYBOARD PERCUSSION
Solo

By JOHN WILLIAMS
Arranged by MICHAEL SWEENEY

RAIDERS MARCH

KEYBOARD PERCUSSION
Band Arrangement

By JOHN WILLIAMS
Arranged by MICHAEL SWEENEY

00860022

From APOLLO 13
APOLLO 13
(End Credits)

KEYBOARD PERCUSSION
Solo

By JAMES HORNER
Arranged by MICHAEL SWEENEY

MCA music publishing

APOLLO 13

(End Credits)

KEYBOARD PERCUSSION
Band Arrangement

By JAMES HORNER
Arranged by MICHAEL SWEENEY

00860022

MCA music publishing

From The Universal Picture E.T. (THE EXTRA-TERRESTRIAL)

THEME FROM E.T. (THE EXTRA-TERRESTRIAL)

KEYBOARD PERCUSSION
Solo

Music by JOHN WILLIAMS
Arranged by MICHAEL SWEENEY

00860022

MCA music publishing

THEME FROM E.T. (THE EXTRA-TERRESTRIAL)

KEYBOARD PERCUSSION
Band Arrangement

Music by JOHN WILLIAMS
Arranged by MICHAEL SWEENEY

MCA music publishing

00860022

Theme From The Paramount Picture STAR TREK

STAR TREK®-THE MOTION PICTURE

KEYBOARD PERCUSSION
Solo

Music by JERRY GOLDSMITH
Arranged by MICHAEL SWEENEY

00860022

STAR TREK®-THE MOTION PICTURE

KEYBOARD PERCUSSION
Band Arrangement

Music by **JERRY GOLDSMITH**
Arranged by **MICHAEL SWEENEY**

From The Universal Motion Picture BACK TO THE FUTURE

BACK TO THE FUTURE

KEYBOARD PERCUSSION
Solo

By ALAN SILVESTRI
Arranged by MICHAEL SWEENEY

MCA music publishing

BACK TO THE FUTURE

KEYBOARD PERCUSSION
Band Arrangement

By ALAN SILVESTRI
Arranged by MICHAEL SWEENEY

00860022

MCA music publishing